The Br

from confetti.co.uk
don't get married without us...

First published in 2003 by Octopus Publishing Group,
2–4 Heron Quays, London, E14 4JP
www.conran-octopus.co.uk
Reprinted in 2004, 2005

A catalogue record for this book is available
from the British Library.

ISBN 1 84091 304 5

Publishing Director Lorraine Dickey
Senior Editor Katey Day
Assistant Editor Sybella Marlow
Creative Director Leslie Harrington
Designer Victoria Burley
Senior Production Controller Manjit Sihra

Contents

THE BRIDESMAID'S WEDDING

Did you know that the role of the bridesmaid dates from pagan times, when evil spirits were thought to attend wedding ceremonies? By surrounding the bride with 'look-a-likes' – similarly dressed attendants of her own age – it was thought the evil ones would not be able to single out the bride.

And frankly, in that fuchsia taffeta horror the bride forced you into, you'd frighten the devil himself…

Only kidding! Being asked to be chief bridesmaid is an honour and most modern brides will at least let you influence the style of your dress, if not the colour.

Also, it's a great excuse to spend months shopping with the bride and to get really involved in her wedding day.

Who should be a bridesmaid?

WHO SHOULD BE A BRIDESMAID?

Who gets the job

Bridesmaids are supposed to be, but are not always, unmarried.

They are usually members of the bride's family, a sister, stepsister, or half-sister, a favourite niece or close friend.

Chief or matron?

The chief bridesmaid is the leader of the pack and is not usually a child, since the job comes with certain duties and responsibilities. If a married woman is chosen as chief bridesmaid, then she is known by the somewhat pompous title of matron of honour.

WHO SHOULD BE A BRIDESMAID?

The best woman

Sometimes the most important bridesmaid is known as the best woman and she is as important to the bride as the best man is to the groom. A bride may also choose to have pageboys and a ring bearer. But it is important for her to have at least one older attendant to help her through the day.

THE BRIDESMAID'S WEDDING

A bridesmaid should be:

Organized – the bridesmaid is meant to look after the bride, not vice versa!

Calm – no matter what disasters may occur, she should be ready to deal with them or divert the bride.

Enthusiastic – there's nothing worse than a bridesmaid who couldn't care less.

WHO SHOULD BE A BRIDESMAID?

A bridesmaid should be:

Focused – a bridesmaid who is too busy looking after her family or chasing the best man on the day is no help at all.

Co-operative – rowing about the colour or cut of her own dress will only add to the overall stress.

Supportive – for when the napkins are the wrong shade of beige or the last pink Rolls Royce is already booked.

Refusing the role

Although it's an honour to be asked, there
are occasions when someone has to refuse.
Acceptable reasons for this are:

- Pregnancy
- A prior engagement on that day
- A previous liaison with the groom
- Illness or disability
- You don't know the bride that well and
are not sure why you've been asked (but
don't state this as your excuse!)

WHO SHOULD BE A BRIDESMAID?

Refusing the role

Unacceptable reasons for refusing are:

- A burning hatred of the groom
- You don't like the bride's dress
- You get a better offer later on for the date of the wedding day
- You can't afford it
- You can't be bothered to help the bride with the organizing

Accepting the role

Once you've accepted, it is important that the bride feels that she can rely on you for ongoing support and to share in the wedding planning.

WHO SHOULD BE A BRIDESMAID?

Accepting the role

If you think you feel doubtful, refuse straight away, before lots of money has been spent and it's too late for the bride to ask anyone else.

The chief bridesmaid

Lean on me

The chief bridesmaid has a vital role in all preparations leading up to the day and plays a supporting role to the bride throughout the wedding day itself.

Here's a guide to what you can expect to have to do…

Six months before

You can expect to be involved in discussions and decisions in the planning stages and to be used as a sounding board for the bride's ideas right from the start.

Six months before

Your main duty is to be the bride's personal assistant: someone she can rely on to chase quotes if required or to calm her down when stress gets the better of her.

An important task for any chief bridesmaid is to be an honest and reliable critic when it comes to choosing the bride's dress. Make sure she gives you some idea of what she is looking for. Then be constructive about the styles and colours that suit her.

Outfits

Along with helping the bride select her dress, as chief bridesmaid you should be involved in choosing outfits for yourself and the other attendants. Ask the bride to tell you the colours and styles she is thinking of, and the ages of her attendants. You should also help with getting the other attendants to fittings on time.

Outfits

Some brides choose older bridesmaids, others like to ask children. Whichever she chooses, you will need to help make sure that they all know what is required of them and what responsibilities they may have.

Outfits

Who pays for the bridesmaids' dresses is a matter of some debate. Traditionally, bridesmaids were provided with material from which they made a dress to their own design. The bride could only dictate the colour, the rest was down to them to make whatever suited best.

Outfits

Modern brides are keen to be more coordinated and most want to have some control over the outfits. In this case, and particularly if the dresses will not be worn again, the bride or her family should pay.

However, parents do sometimes pay for their children's clothes and older bridesmaids might help out with the cost of their dresses.

Four months before

If the bride is trying out a new beauty or fitness regime before the wedding, your support will be very welcome! If she's going to aerobics or has taken up jogging, try to go along to keep up morale.

Four months before

Having a makeover is a fun way to spend a morning or afternoon. Try out some new brands or make-up artists for the big day and see what suits you, or just plain enjoy yourselves doing something girlie!

Four months before

You might be asked to act as an intermediary if differences of opinion occur, perhaps between the bride and her parents or parents-in-law. Fingers crossed this won't be necessary, but disagreements do happen from time to time.

Four months before

This might be a good time to check with the bride's other attendants to make sure that they've made the necessary arrangements for their outfits, and that they know when the wedding rehearsals are, if asked to attend.

Two months before

One of your more fun duties is to arrange the hen night celebrations. This could be anything from an evening in a restaurant to an action-packed weekend away.

Two months before

The hen night is supposed to be a surprise for the bride but, always check before if she has any 'no go' areas, such as muscle-bound strippergrams, for example!

Although these are usually fun, you won't want the star of the evening to feel uncomfortable on her own hen night when it could have been avoided.

Two months before

Ask the bride to give you a list of who she wants to invite, as it is unlikely that you will know all of her friends.

(See The hen night on page 42 for more advice and ideas).

Two months before

If the bride is having a dinner for her hen night, or you are throwing her an American-style bridal shower, you will probably be expected to make a speech, so now's the time to start thinking about what you might say.

Two months before

Now's the time to encourage the bride to start a course of facials, manicures and pedicures so she'll look her best on the day. (And of course, you'll benefit as well...) Book an appointment with her hairdresser so you can both try out hairdos.

Two months before

The strain of the wedding planning may be getting to the bride at this point so make sure she keeps calm and relaxed.
The Wedding Book of Calm might be just the thing to give her, for last-minute tips on staying frazzle-free.

One week before

As chief bridesmaid you should attend the wedding rehearsal so that you know where you and the other attendants should stand, when you should sit down and the exact order of the ceremony.

If the couple have a dinner after their wedding rehearsal, it is also traditional for you to toast them then.

One week before

Phone all the other attendants to make sure no one's suffering from last-minute nerves or problems that they're too nervous or embarrassed to speak to the bride about. Check in with the best man. Don't forget yourself too. There's nothing worse than spending all your time ensuring the bride looks beautiful and all the attendants are happy, only to discover at the last minute that your underwear is uncomfortable or that you can't find your shoes!

The day before the wedding

If circumstances allow, you may want to spend the day or evening with the bride, especially if she's nervous or spending the night apart from the groom.

Also, you should both have your bridal manicure today.

The day before the wedding

Now that hen nights are no longer usually
held the night before the wedding, it's a
great opportunity to have a quiet evening
in with some videos and a glass of wine
and have a good chat! Encourage her to
talk about what she thinks tomorrow will
mean to her – the day itself will go so
fast it's a good idea to get some of
the contemplation in beforehand!

Pre-wedding checklist

Emergency kit:
Tights
Tissues
Baby wipes
Breath mints
Safety pins
Comb/brush
Lipstick

THE CHIEF BRIDESMAID

Pre-wedding checklist

Nail file

Hair grips

Hair spray

Spare earring backs

Mobile phone (switched off)

Pain relief tablets

Pen

Pre-wedding checklist

Pack the emergency kit in a bag and leave
it in the car to pick up after the ceremony.
If the bride loses the back of her earring
or a guest breaks a strap on her dress,
you'll be able to rush to the rescue.

Confetti

Make sure the wedding guests have plenty of confetti – if allowed – and that they know when they can throw it.

Choose from 70 different kinds at
www.confetti.co.uk/shopping/default.asp

The hen night

A night to remember

Today's hen nights have to cater for a wider audience, so there's much more variety on offer. They're less about strippers and L-plates – unless that's what you're all up for – and more about originality and style.

Supply on demand

Brides can have as many as three hen nights nowadays: one with work colleagues, during the week; one suitable for all audiences, including granny; and one big blow-out.

It's up to you to find out whether the bride and her friends are expecting a weekend in Ibiza or a cream tea in St Ives and plan accordingly. Remember the bride's likes and dislikes as a general guide for letting your creativity and party planning skills run free!

Check it out

For more ideas and contact details of all kinds of hen night activities, check out the Supplier Directory on confetti.co.uk: www.confetti.co.uk/confetti_pages /default.asp

You'll find great places to stay in the venue finder too: www.confetti.co.uk/venues/default.asp

When to hold it

Despite tradition, it's not now generally considered a good idea to have the hen party the night before the big day. Ideally, hold it two weeks before the wedding or, even better, during the same weekend as the groom's stag night, as this means the couple have as many free weekends together as possible during the run up to the wedding.

Who pays?

It's usual for everyone to pay for themselves and to all chip in to cover the bride too. It's less hassle to ask everyone to contribute towards a kitty before you go out. If you're spending a weekend away, avoid having to chase up payments after the event by telling everyone you can't reserve their place unless they give you a cheque in advance.

For clubbers

If you want to rave the night away, bear in mind that many clubs have a strict door policy, so phone your chosen club in advance to check you're welcome – and ask if they offer group discounts. Alternatively, book a party bus tour of London nightclubs – one price should cover all wine and beer available on the bus, plus entry fees into clubs.

For beauty queens

Many companies offer a service where they will send a representative or two to your home for a makeover. Reflexologists and aromatherapists will also make home visits.

For action girls

Have fun with a day's paintballing or dry slope skiing – or if the budget's tight, organize a game of volleyball or rounders in a local park followed by pints in a nearby pub.

For modern couples

Take inspiration from Sophie and Edward,
who opted for a joint hen and stag night;
they invited ten friends each for a weekend
at a country house, to ride and play ball!
If you're not related to anyone on the civil
list, however, you and the best man could
cook a meal at your home or his and invite
the happy couple and guests for dinner and
silly board games.

For party animals

Pack your bags for a mad weekend of partying! The best places to head for include Amsterdam, Barcelona and Dublin.

Get quotes from travel agents to give everyone a costing before they decide to commit themselves.

For party animals

Once you've got a firm number, ask everyone for full payment before booking.

During the summer months there are any number of festivals on around the UK, simply choose your favourite kind of music, pack a tent and enjoy!

For artistic temperaments

Glaze-your-own-pottery places are popular
and make a really fun hen night alternative
where you create your own souvenirs!
Many places will lay on wine and nibbles
for a hen party booking.

For gamblers

Organize a night at the dogs or set up a mini casino at home. Several companies can supply gaming tables, accessories, croupiers and funny money for an authentic touch! For an ultimate weekend of gambling, fly out to Las Vegas on Friday afternoon. It doesn't matter what time you arrive because this is a 24-hour city and there are no 'last orders'.

For culture vultures

Head to a city such as Oxford to wander around the dreaming spires, visit the museums and colleges and take a punt down the river. Or disappear to Cornwall for such often missed gems as Tate St Ives and the Eden Project as well as delicious scrumpy in local hostelries!

THE HEN NIGHT

For traditionalists

Make for Blackpool or Brighton for a stage show featuring either attractive naked men or men dressed as women, before hitting a local nightclub. If you're staying at home, an Ann Summers party is just the thing!

For bliss-seekers

Hen weekends don't have to be about getting sozzled. Why not visit a spa retreat or health farm? Book yourselves in for massage therapy so you'll all be completely relaxed come the big day. If you can't make a whole weekend, go for a day or ask someone with membership to a nice gym to help out.

Horses for courses

Don't just stop at a day at the races, go for
the double! Combine Chester and Aintree,
Lingfield and Epsom or Doncaster and York
to give yourself twice as many opportunities
of winning enough cash to cover all those
last minute wedding expenses.

Hen night games

Quizzes are always a good way to get the party moving. Confetti's book *Wedding Trivia* is a good standby here, with loads of wedding and romance-related questions to test the bride. Make an evening out of it with wine and nibbles and see just how well you score!

Hen night games

Or make your own quiz based on her
career or personality or that of her future
husband. For instance, a trainee teacher
could be tested on the subject she is
meant to teach or a doctor could have
to identify parts of the body from
bad photocopies!

Blue rinse

Have a quiz where the questions are a bit more saucy. Play 'I Have Never', where one person claims they 'have never done/said something' saucy, and anyone who has done or said that thing must have a drink. Play 'Truth or Dare' where each participant is asked a question that she can either answer truthfully or choose to fulfil a dare instead. Dares can be relatively tame, from asking the best-looking man in the room to dance with you, to singing on the pavement till you make a pound!

Caught on film

And don't forget to take a camera. Apart
from anything else, some of those photos
might be invaluable fodder for the chief
bridesmaid's speech…

For great value disposable cameras with
online prints, see

www.confetti.co.uk/shopping/default.asp

Wedding day duties

Best friend, best woman

As chief bridesmaid, your role on the day is of utmost importance to the bride and the other attendants. You must maintain a calming influence throughout the day and be as organized as possible.

Here are your main duties on the day to ensure everything runs smoothly…

Before setting off

Ensure that everyone is where they should be when they should be, that the right clothes and accessories are ready for the right person, and that you are prepared to deal with any emergencies that might arise.

Before setting off

Your other duties on the day include:
arriving at the bride's house in plenty of
time for the hairdresser and make-up
artist; being on hand to help dress younger
attendants and keep them looking perfect
until the transport arrives; looking after
emergency supplies – lipstick, tissues,
etc – for the bride throughout the day.

Before setting off

You will probably travel to the ceremony venue with the bride's mum and the other attendants. Your calming influence may be tested to the limit, as everyone will be excited and perhaps a little emotional about the coming events.

At the ceremony venue

Once all the attendants are assembled, the photographer may want to take some pictures before the bride arrives. You will have to organize the other bridesmaids and pageboys, particularly any very young ones.

At the ceremony venue

When the bride arrives, ensure everyone is assembled and in the right position behind her, ready for her entrance. Calm any excited little bridesmaids and pageboys using bribery if necessary.

WEDDING DAY DUTIES

At the ceremony venue

Make any necessary adjustments to the bride's veil and dress so that she looks absolutely gorgeous for her big entrance as all eyes will be on her and that fabulous dress.

During the ceremony

Bridesmaids have very specific duties. You will follow the bride into the venue (or you may go first, American style) and usually sit near the front, ready for the procession at the end. Make sure that you know where to go and that any very young children have their parents close by.

During the ceremony

Once the bride has joined the groom, as chief bridesmaid you should take her bouquet and gloves, if she is wearing any, and look after them for the duration of the service.

During the ceremony

If in a church, when the couple sign the
register, go with them into the vestry or
side room, accompanied by the best man,
to witness the signing.

During the ceremony

On leaving the ceremony venue, you as the chief bridesmaid and the best man take your positions behind the bride and her new husband for the recessional.

Other older bridesmaids will be escorted by the ushers. Younger bridesmaids and pageboys will follow behind.

Immediately after the ceremony

Once you are all outside, you may need to organize the couple and attendants for the photographs. It is also quite usual for you to have your photo taken with the best man.

Next, gather together any runaway younger attendants and get them all into the car to take them to the reception.

At the reception

Once at the reception, the bride may want you to be a part of the receiving line. The purpose of the line is to allow the guests to meet the bridal party, and to ensure that the bride and groom say at least a few words to each guest.

At the reception

You may have the responsibility for displaying the bride's bouquet somewhere safe (and preferably cool), ensuring it doesn't get damaged during the rest of the day. This is especially important if she is planning to have the flowers preserved.

At the reception

You should also circulate amongst the guests during the reception, ensuring that they are enjoying themselves and using any disposable cameras provided. In this way you act as the bride's back-up; she will have only limited time to spend with each guest.

At the reception

Although the speeches at the reception are generally a male prerogative, it is becoming more usual for either the bride, chief bridesmaid, or even both of you to make a speech.

At the reception

If, as chief bridesmaid, you are to make a speech, then you should plan early and have a clear idea of the sentiments you wish to express (see The speech, page 84, for more advice and ideas).

Evening reception

The first dance is exclusively reserved for the newlyweds, but it is traditional for the chief bridesmaid to take to the floor with the best man and join the happy couple midway through the first dance.

Evening reception

Finally, when the couple change into their going-away outfits, you should be on hand to take care of the bride's dress and ensure that it is returned to her home or, if necessary, to the hire shop. The other attendants' dresses may need to be returned too and she may well ask you to take responsibility for this.

Speak up

Although there is a growing trend for bridesmaids to make speeches, it is neither traditional nor compulsory and will not happen at all weddings. If the bride is making a speech, it is a nice touch for her chief bridesmaid, or best friend or sister, to add a short speech to hers.

Keep it simple and use it to highlight whatever aspects of your friend that you most admire.

Research

If you're stuck for stories or ideas, get together with friends and relatives for reminiscences – they'll be only too delighted to have their say! While they sit there swapping stories, you may find the bulk of your speech will have been written for you by the end of the night.

THE SPEECH

Starting out

Dig out your old photo albums, letters and cuttings and ask for help from friends and family. You might find something funny to read out or use as a prop.

Star gazing

Horoscopes are another good source of material. The star sign of the bride will have associated characteristics and it can be amusing to compare the bride and her sign to see whether the qualities match or not.

Star gazing

Or you can talk about what the stars have in store for the bride and groom by charting their future.

For other ideas, see *Compatibility* from the confetti.co.uk series.

Name games

Looking at the couple's names, researching the origins, and revealing their true meaning is a great way of finding material to start a speech.

Name games

Also check out *How to Write a Wedding Speech* and *Wedding Speeches* from the confetti.co.uk series – a gold-mine of ways to start and end your speech in style!

Delivering your speech

If you're having difficulty knowing how to begin, you could consider using an anecdote about something that has happened during the day, or a comment that a guest made earlier to you or in passing about the day's event.

Delivering your speech

These do not necessarily have to be true. If you say 'someone said to me earlier that...' no one will know who the 'someone' was and whether it was actually said. This also means that you do not need to pin a comment on any one guest.

Sample speech

Some suggested openings for a chief bridesmaid's speech will follow. While they may not be relevant to your situation, they can serve as a starting point.

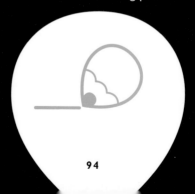

Sample speech

I would just like to take this opportunity to say a heartfelt thank you to Abby [bride] for giving me the honour of being her chief bridesmaid...

Sample speech

You may think that you have heard everything that needs to be said, but I haven't even started yet. Don't despair though, I am not the stereotypical woman who you men think can talk forever on any subject... although weddings have become a speciality of mine over the past twelve months...

Sample speech

*We have all heard the lovely compliments paid
to the bridesmaids in the speeches and
I thank Robert [best man] for this on
their behalf. I would like to return the
compliment and say how very handsome
the groomsmen all look today in their
morning suits...*

Speech checklist

- Do compliment the bride and thank her for choosing you as chief bridesmaid

- Do comment on the preparations for the wedding that you have organized together

Speech checklist

• Do compliment the ushers on behalf of the bridesmaids

• Do remember that the bride's family and work colleagues may be at the wedding, so avoid any scandalous revelations or mentions of how much she hates her job!

Speech checklist

- Don't refer to past relationships of either the bride or groom. The reference may be funny in private conversation, but it would be unwise to use it as material for a speech aimed at a family audience

Speech checklist

- Don't refer to anything the groom does not know about and that could cause unnecessary embarrassment

- Do toast the bride and groom

Young bridesmaids and pageboys

What about the littlest bridesmaids?

Young bridesmaids and pageboys make a beautiful addition to the bridal party, and their uninhibited and natural behaviour can provide amusement and some relief from the tensions of the day.

Here is a guide to their responsibilities and what will be expected of them.

Parental permission

When considering who to choose check first with the child's parents to see if the child will be available and happy to do it.

Small outfits, big costs

Whether or not the parents should contribute to the cost of the outfits is a tricky dilemma. It's important that this is discussed as soon as possible.

It's far better to agree a compromise during the early stages than to risk a misunderstanding because this hadn't been discussed at the very beginning.

The terrible twos

Age is an important factor when choosing these attendants, as while very young bridesmaids and pageboys may look delightful, they could end up being fidgety and are often reluctant to perform to cue.

The way to a child's heart

This is where you, the chief bridesmaid, come into your own, armed with a small bag of treats to encourage good behaviour. Parents of younger children may need to be roped in to help too.

Things to consider

Although the main function of the little
ones is to add to the general beauty and
delight of the day, as everyone knows,
angelic smiles can sometimes hide a heart
of stone when it comes to coaxing them
into smart clothes.

Things to consider

To stand a chance of getting what they do
to coincide with what they should do,
read the following pages aloud to any
prospective bridesmaids and pageboys…

Looking the part

Your main job, if you are chosen, is to take part in the bridal procession when the bride and groom actually get married, and to be in the photos. The bride will have a picture in her mind of how she wants everyone to look on the day. Bridesmaids usually wear a mini-version of the dresses the adult bridesmaids will wear or something that fits in with the theme or the colour of the rest of the outfits.

Looking the part

Pageboys often have sailor suits, waistcoats or quite fancy get-ups. Whatever the outfit is like, remember that clothes not only have to look good on, but also match with everyone else. So even if you don't like your outfit, when you see it next to everyone else's, it will fit in really well.

And playing the part

Throwing a tantrum because you don't like the height of your heels or pattern of your waistcoat won't make you anybody's friend!

It's also a good idea to go to the toilet before you go to the place where the wedding is being held!

And playing the part

Frankly there's no point getting dressed up
like a Christmas tree if you're going to
spend the day fidgeting around, suddenly
becoming shy, picking your nose or
generally making a nuisance of yourself.

And playing the part

If you think you might get bored, or not be able to follow what is going on, don't worry. Ceremonies usually last about half an hour, and there is often a leaflet that will tell you what is going to happen next. Quite often people will get up and do readings or you will all sing hymns.

And playing the part

The most important bit of the day is when the couple make their wedding vows. This is what you're all here to see, so make sure you're paying attention when it happens. Sometimes there will be a rehearsal before the wedding day, just like your school play!

On the day itself

Generally you will get ready at the bride's home before travelling to the wedding with the chief bridesmaid. Or perhaps your parents might take you instead.

Once you've arrived, it's time to wait (patiently!) for the bride to arrive.

It's traditional for the bride to be a bit late, so be prepared for that.

On the day itself

Once she's there, you'll follow the bride
to where the priest or registrar is standing.
During the ceremony you'll either sit with
the bride or with your parents – check
where you'll be before you go in.

Photographs

This is no time to be camera shy!
You'll be required to pose for photographs
on your own and with other people.
After this, you'll make your way to the
reception – that's the party that follows a
wedding – with your parents or the
chief bridesmaid.

At the reception

Usually you won't have any duties so you can just enjoy the party! There will be food, speeches and then dancing. It's a good idea to pay attention during the speeches, even if you think they're dull, because if the bride and groom are going to thank you, this is when they'll do it. If there are other children at the wedding you'll probably sit with them; if it's mostly grown-ups then you might sit with your parents, or whoever brought you to the wedding.

Flower girls

The flower girl tends to be a very young
bridesmaid, who walks down the aisle in
front of everyone else during the wedding
ceremony. She gets her name because she
sometimes scatters petals or confetti on
the ground for the bride to walk on, and
sometimes hands out confetti for people
to throw after the ceremony.

Flower girls

Often she is dressed as a flower fairy, or sometimes in the same colours as the bridesmaids. She can sit with her parents during the wedding.

Ring bearer

Sometimes the bride and groom ask one of their attendants, usually a pageboy, to be their ring bearer.

Ring bearer

If you're asked to be a ring bearer, you'll carry a cushion with the rings on, which you will pass to the bride and groom when it is time for them to exchange wedding rings. It's up to the best man to give you those precious rings before the ceremony, so make sure you talk to him before it starts.

Thank you

Finally, this is an exciting day for everyone
involved and, as you've had a very
important role to perform in helping the
day run smoothly, you will be mentioned
in the speeches.

Thank you

Traditionally it is the groom's place to compliment and thank you in his speech. It's often the groom's responsibility to present you with a small thank you gift too.

Final words of wisdom

If you're a bridesmaid, whether you're 5 or 50, remember the main thing is to enjoy it all – the preparation, the anticipation, the day itself. After all, it's not every day that someone close to you gets married and asks for your help, so take the time to get involved and have fun!

Final words of wisdom

If you need inspiration or advice,
www.confetti.co.uk is available 24 hours
a day for you to get all the information
you need, and is the place to buy all those
hen night and party necessities.
You can even chat to others on our
message boards.

ABOUT CONFETTI.CO.UK

Confetti.co.uk is the UK's leading weddings and special occasion website, helping more than 300,000 brides, grooms and guests every month.

To find out more or to order your confetti gift book, party brochure or wedding stationery brochure, visit www.confetti.co.uk email info@confetti.co.uk

visit Confetti, 80 Tottenham Court Road, London W1 or call 0870 840 6060

Some of the other books in this comprehensive series: *The Best Man's Wedding*, *Your Daughter's Wedding*, *Men At Weddings*, and *Wedding Planner*